YOUR VICTORY IN THE MAKING

A 30 DAY DEVOTIONAL

LUCIA M. CLABORN

ISBN 978-1-7372116-62

Your Victory In The Making - A 30-Day Devotional
By Lucia M. Claborn
Copyright © 2020 by Lucia M. Claborn
All rights reserved.
Published in the United States of America.
Lucia M. Claborn, LLC
2586 County Road 165,
Moulton, Alabama 35650
www.LuciaClaborn.com

Dedication

This devotional is lovingly dedicated to you.

As you read through the pages of this devotional, my prayer is that you will renew your mind with God's Word, ponder on the thoughts, answer the questions, and receive a greater revelation that God created you to walk in total victory in every area of your life regardless of what your life appears to be like right now.

God loves you and has a greater level of victory on His mind for you to enjoy and experience in your life today.

Never doubt God's mighty power to work in you and accomplish all this. He will achieve infinitely more than your greatest request, your most unbelievable dream, and exceed your wildest imagination! He will outdo them all, for his miraculous power constantly energizes you. - Ephesians 3:20

Table of Contents

Acknowledgements

Projects such as this do not just come into existence, there are always those behind the scenes making things happen. I would like to thank those dear to my heart that helped make this dream a reality.

Tanya Tenica Patxot, my activation coach. There are not enough words to express my gratitude for you investing yourself into activating me to pursue my dreams. I thank God for bringing you to me to help birth my dreams. Everything God brought you through was specifically for me. You inspire me to not quit or give up. Thank you.

Judith Taylor, my editor, and publisher. You are such a vital part of making my dreams a reality and I would not want to be on this adventure with anyone else. Thank you for doing what you do to make my projects come to life. I appreciate your kindness and your affirmations to ensure everything is just part of the process. Thank you.

Linda Starks, my friend, my sister, my prayer warrior, and my intercessor. Thank you for the countless hours you spend covering my business, my projects and myself in prayer. You have averted countless enemy attacks in my life, and you are priceless to me. Thank you.

Introduction

By living in God, love has been brought to its full expression in us so that we may fearlessly face the day of judgment, because all that Jesus now is, so are we in this world.
1 John 4:17

God created you in His image and He has a wonderful plan for you. This plan includes enforcing Satan's defeat and walking in victory every day of your life.

Victory is not something you are striving to achieve, you already possess victory. As a child of God, you are everything that Jesus is. Since He is seated in the place of victory at the right hand of Father God, far above all powers and principalities, and wickedness in high places, that is where you are seated also.

Although you are seated in the place of victory, victory does not just automatically happen. You must build your faith with the Word of God to receive everything Jesus has already paid the price for you to enjoy while you are here on earth.

If you want to be a victorious champion, I encourage you to read through the pages of this devotional and linger with Holy Spirit to allow Him to reveal God's heart for you and the love He has for you. Don't rush through the pages.

To build your faith to walk in victory, read each scripture out loud and imagine God is speaking directly to you. Add your name to the verse to make it personal as you read it. Allow Holy Spirit to affirm to you that God created you to live victoriously. Let Him guide you into victory in every area of your life.

Meditate the scriptures, mull them over in your mind, answer the questions with new revelations from Father God so you can go to the next level of victory.

As you begin your journey through this devotional to build your faith for victory in every area of your life, the prayer I pray for you is from Ephesians 1:17-23: *I pray that the Father of glory, the God of our Lord Jesus Christ, would impart to you the riches of the Spirit of wisdom and the Spirit of revelation to know him through your deepening intimacy with him.*

I pray that the light of God will illuminate the eyes of your imagination, flooding you with light, until you experience the full revelation of the hope of his calling —that is, the wealth of God's glorious inheritances that he finds in us, his holy ones!

I pray that you will continually experience the immeasurable greatness of God's power made available to you through faith. Then your lives will be an advertisement of this immense power as it works through you! This is the mighty power that was released when God raised Christ from the dead and exalted him to the place of highest honor and supreme authority in the heavenly realm! And now he is exalted as first above every ruler, authority, government, and realm of power in existence! He is gloriously enthroned over every name that is ever praised, not only in this age, but in the age that is coming!

And he alone is the leader and source of everything needed in the church. God has put everything beneath the authority of Jesus Christ and has given him the highest rank above all others. And now we, his church, are his body on the earth and that which fills him who is being filled by it!

Day 1

You Have Conquered The World

Little children, you can be certain that you belong to God and have conquered them, for the One who is living in you is far greater than the one who is in the world. 1 John 4:4

My child, how I love you. You belong to me. I am your loving Father. I created you and I know every detail about you and your life. I experience your joys, your victories, your pains, your disappointments, and I know your thoughts.

I made you an overcomer. I constructed you to be a conqueror in your life. You are not designed to live a defeated life. You are fabricated to rise above and conquer every attack of Satan, who is your true enemy, because I am living on the inside of you.

The same Spirit that created the world when I spoke it into existence is the same Spirit that raised My Son Jesus from the dead. This same Spirit, My Holy Spirit, lives on the inside of you.

Do you realize who is living inside you as my child? You have creative, resurrection power living on the inside of you to help you every moment of every day so you can conquer the world and walk in victory!

Prayer - *Thank you, Father God that I am your child, and you know every detail of my life. Please help me realize and be more aware that the Holy Spirit lives on the inside of me. He is my Helper. The Holy Spirit help me realize you have already won the victory over the enemy for me because you are in me and more powerful than anything in this world.*

Thoughts to Ponder.

You not only have access to God's Word that is full of creative power when you speak it out, you also have the Holy Spirit living on the inside of you. Plus, you have a Covenant of the Favor of God on your life! You are made in the image of God, Jesus, and the Holy Spirit - you can overcome everything this world throws at you and walk in victory. Holy Spirit is leading you.

Taking Action For Victory.

What is one thing from this verse that God is affirming to you right now?

_____

_____

_____

After meditating on this verse, how does it inspire you to re-evaluate your faith journey so you can walk in victory?

_____

_____

_____

How will you apply this verse to your life so you can begin walking in victory or rise to a higher level of victory in your life?

_____

_____

_____

Day 2

You Triumph Over Everything

Yet even in the midst of all these things, we triumph over them all, for God has made us to be more than conquerors, and his demonstrated love is our glorious victory over everything! Romans 8:37

My child, you may be encountering various troubles, persecutions, pressures, dangers, or problems in your life today. However, they do not isolate you from My love. Actually, there is nothing in this world that can separate you from My love.

If you are experiencing these things, remember Jesus triumphed over all of them. My love makes you more than a conqueror because no situation in your life can defeat you or dilute My love for you. My divine love and power work for you to triumph over everything in this world. You share in the victory spoils of every enemy you face today.

You captured My heart with your love with a glance of your worshiping eyes. My love gives you "a glorious hyper-victory," more than can be described or can be contained in one word. My love and grace have made you a hyper-conqueror, empowered to be unrivaled, and more than a match for any enemy! I made you to live a hyper-victorious lifestyle every day!

Prayer - *Lord, thank You that I am created to live a hyper-victorious life. Nothing can separate me from Your love. Thank You that Jesus paid the price for me to live victoriously. Father, I ask You in Jesus Name to help me walk in a greater awareness of Your love so I can love others. I decree because Jesus walked in victory, I walk in victory.*

Thoughts to Ponder.

You may have pressure or signs of the enemy's attack in your life today; however, every circumstance is subject to change. As you allow God to pour His love out on you and you receive His love, your love walk will be perfected and you will walk in a higher level of victory because your faith works by love.

Taking Action For Victory.

What is one thing from this verse that God is affirming to you right now?

_____

_____

_____

After meditating on this verse, how does it inspire you to re-evaluate your faith journey so you can walk in victory?

_____

_____

_____

How will you apply this verse to your life so you can begin walking in victory or rise to a higher level of victory in your life?

_____

_____

_____

Day 3

You Are A Chosen Treasure

But you are God's chosen treasure — priests who are kings, a spiritual "nation" set apart as God's devoted ones. He called you out of darkness to experience his marvelous light, and now he claims you as his very own. He did this so that you would broadcast his glorious wonders throughout the world.
1 Peter 2:9

Do you realize you are my treasure, a precious, rare gem? My child, how I love you. You belong to Me. I am your loving Father. I created you for relationship with Me and I know every detail about you and your life. I experience your joys, your victories, your pains, your disappointments, and I know your every thought.

I made you an overcomer. I constructed you to be a conqueror. You are not designed to live a life of defeat. I am calling you out of darkness into My glorious light.

You are fabricated to rise above and conquer every attack of Satan, your true enemy, because I am living within you.

You have creative, resurrection power living inside you to help you every moment of every day to walk in victory! As you overcome life's challenges through My power, you will naturally want to share My goodness to you with the world.

Prayer - *Thank You, Lord, for choosing me to be Your heart's treasure, and for calling me out of darkness into Your marvelous light. I decree I am Yours. I belong to You. I ask You to give me greater revelation of Your power that's available to me. I receive all Your goodness today. I am telling my world of Your glorious wonders.*

Thoughts to Ponder.

You are a special treasure to God. He describes you as a place where "guarded wealth" is stored. This is an indication that you are a safe place for the king's jewels, or treasures, because they have extraordinary value. God calls you a priest and king, His unique and special treasure of great importance. You are a treasure above all other treasures.

Taking Action For Victory.

What is one thing from this verse that God is affirming to you right now?

_____

_____

_____

After meditating on this verse, how does it inspire you to re-evaluate your faith journey so you can walk in victory?

_____

_____

_____

How will you apply this verse to your life so you can begin walking in victory or rise to a higher level of victory in your life?

_____

_____

_____

Day 4

God Keeps His Promises To You

So now, wrap your heart tightly around the hope that lives within us, knowing that God always keeps his promises!
Hebrews 10:23

My dearest child, I am here for you and with you. I always keep My promises to you. You can trust Me, in that if I told you I would do something for you, I will do it. I will not disappoint you.

I get blamed for many things that I do not do. I ask you to see Me as your Good Daddy; a kind and loving Father that only wants to do good to you and for you. Although things may not always go the way you have them planned, I want to remind you that all of My plans for you are wonderfully good. I will not harm you. I want to give you hope for a bright and prosperous future. I promise you; I am worthy of your trust.

I am not a man that I would lie to you. I encourage you to find My promises to you in My Word for your situation. When you read My Love Letters to you, you will see that when I tell you that you can have something, you can have it. You can put your hope and trust in Me. I am always faithful to you.

Will you put your hope and trust in Me today so I can lead you into your victory? I will do it for you!

Prayer - *Lord, I ask You to help me stir up my hope because it is the anchor of my soul. This anchor is what my faith attaches itself to so Your promise will manifest in my life. I ask You to help me believe Your word and trust You when You tell me that all Your plans for my life are good, and You only want to prosper me.*

Thoughts to Ponder.

The hope within your heart is the anchor upon which your faith attaches itself to until you see your desired promise from the Word of God become a reality in your life. God will never disappoint you as you keep your eyes on Him and stand on His promises. One promise from His Word is all you need to stand on until you see your promise manifested.

Taking Action For Victory.

What is one thing from this verse that God is affirming to you right now?

_____

_____

_____

After meditating on this verse, how does it inspire you to re-evaluate your faith journey so you can walk in victory?

_____

_____

_____

How will you apply this verse to your life so you can begin walking in victory or rise to a higher level of victory in your life?

_____

_____

_____

Day 5

No Weapon Will Harm You

"But I promise you, no weapon meant to hurt you will succeed, and you will refute every accusing word spoken against you. This promise is the inheritance of Yahweh's servants, and their vindication is from me," says Yahweh.
Isaiah 54:17

My darling child, do you sense the enemy's fiery darts attacking you? Do you hear the accuser's relentless accusations against you swirling in your mind?

I am here to assure you that these weapons will not harm you or defeat you. Gaze upon Me. Put your focus on My Word.

As My child, I created you to walk in victory over Satan's allegations and lies. You have power to condemn every word spoken against you. You must answer accusing lies of the enemy with promises from My Word.

Rise up and take your place of authority because you are My chosen child. Victory is your inheritance. Raise your head up as a champion. Use your weapons of warfare from My Word to answer and silence your enemy, which is Satan, the accuser of the brethren. I am your vindicator, and I am defending you.

Prayer - *Lord, I thank You that as Your child I have an inheritance from You. I ask You to vindicate me today. Thank You that no weapon formed against me will hurt me, or prosper in what it was sent to do to harm me. Every tongue that rises against me I will condemn. I decree I am free from the power of the enemy's lies in my life.*

Thoughts to Ponder.

Jesus paid the price for your inheritance of victory and vindication over every lie and attack of Satan because you are God's child. He loves you. The only way you fail in life is by giving up or quitting. To live victoriously, stay in faith by hearing God's Word. Open your mouth, speak out and condemn Satan's lies and accusations with promises from God's Word.

Taking Action For Victory.

What is one thing from this verse that God is affirming to you right now?

_____

_____

_____

After meditating on this verse, how does it inspire you to re-evaluate your faith journey so you can walk in victory?

_____

_____

_____

How will you apply this verse to your life so you can begin walking in victory or rise to a higher level of victory in your life?

_____

_____

_____

Day 6

Living In God's Freedom of Grace

Remember this: sin will not conquer you, for God already has! You are not governed by law but governed by the reign of the grace of God. Romans 6:14

You are My precious child. When you accepted My Son, Jesus, as your Lord and Savior, you became a brand-new person, one that never existed before. Your old sin nature died.

When you were joined to Jesus in baptism, you died as He died, and you rose again to a new life as He rose again to a new life by the resurrection power of the Holy Spirit.

Through your union with Jesus, you no longer live under the Law of Sin and Death, because Jesus fulfilled the Law. You now live under the Covenant of Grace. Sin lost its power over you once and for all.

Therefore, you must no longer give sin opportunity to rule your life, controlling how you live or compelling you to obey its desires and cravings.

Instead, answer sin with My call to keep yielding your body to Me as one who has experienced resurrection life!

Prayer - *Father, I thank You that my old man died with Jesus when I was baptized, and I now have a new nature. I ask You to help me realize I became a brand-new person, one that never existed before, when I rose up with Jesus. Thank You that I am dead to sin and alive to You. Help me remember that I now live under a Covenant of Grace and not under the Law.*

Thoughts to Ponder.

Living under God's Grace is liberating. Grace gives you freedom to choose your master. Choosing to love sin, will reward you with death. Choosing to love and obey God, leads you to perfect righteousness. Now that you live under the Covenant of Grace, you can celebrate your freedom from your former master of sin because Jesus has set you free.

Taking Action For Victory.

What is one thing from this verse that God is affirming to you right now?

_____

_____

_____

After meditating on this verse, how does it inspire you to re-evaluate your faith journey so you can walk in victory?

_____

_____

_____

How will you apply this verse to your life so you can begin walking in victory or rise to a higher level of victory in your life?

_____

_____

_____

Day 7

Receive Your Victor's Crown

If your faith remains strong, even while surrounded by life's difficulties, you will continue to experience the untold blessings of God! True happiness comes as you pass the test with faith, and receive the victorious crown of life promised to every lover of God! James 1:12

Does it seem as though you are facing many difficulties or challenges in your life today? Take a deep breath My child. Can you stop for a moment and consider them as invaluable opportunities to experience great joy!

Know that when your faith is tested it stirs up the power within you to endure situations like those you are facing today. As your endurance, or patience grows stronger, it releases perfection into every part of your life until there is nothing missing, nothing lacking, and you are perfectly complete.

If you lack wisdom while you are waiting patiently, ask Me for a generous supply. I will give it to you without rebuking or condemning you for asking Me for what you need.

When you use your faith to produce results, and then you pass the test, you will receive the victor's crown. There will be nothing lacking or missing in your life.

Prayer - *Lord, I ask You to give me wisdom as I encounter various difficulties and challenges so I can stand strong in my faith. I am asking You to help me endure with great joy so Your patience will have her perfect work in my life. As patience has her perfect work, I will be complete, not lacking anything and I will receive the victor's crown.*

Thoughts to Ponder.

When you are in the middle of difficulties, and feel tempted to give up, do not say, "God is tempting me," because He is incapable of being tempted by evil. He is never the source of your temptation to quit during tests or trials. Instead, ask God to give you wisdom and strength to use your faith to pass the test and win your victor's crown.

Taking Action For Victory.

What is one thing from this verse that God is affirming to you right now?

_____

_____

_____

After meditating on this verse, how does it inspire you to re-evaluate your faith journey so you can walk in victory?

_____

_____

_____

How will you apply this verse to your life so you can begin walking in victory or rise to a higher level of victory in your life?

_____

_____

_____

Day 8

You Are A Victorious Conqueror

But we thank God for giving us the victory as conquerors through our Lord Jesus, the Anointed One. 1 Corinthians 15:57

My little one, do you understand that it is sin that gives death its sting, and it is the Law that empowers sin in your life? The Law says do not do something, which in turn makes you want to do it all the more.

The victory you celebrate is the victory Jesus paid the price for you to enjoy when He died on the cross. Jesus gave you total victory over sin when He rose to life again. The sting of death that Jesus removed is the empowering of sin in your life by the Law.

You have reason to celebrate your victory. Thank Me for making you more than a conqueror through Jesus. He has already given you the victory, so stand firm, stable, and endure with great joy.

Live your life with an unshakable confidence to prosper and excel in every season. You can be assured that your union with Jesus makes your labor produce fruit that endures.

Prayer - *Father, thank You that I am delivered from the Law of sin and death, and I now live under a Covenant of Grace. The sting of sin and death has been defeated in my life. Thank You that You always cause me to triumph like a champion. You have already given me the victory through Jesus Christ, and I believe I receive my victory right now in Jesus Name.*

Thoughts to Ponder.

Although Satan appeared to be the champion at the cross, Jesus defeated him, defeated sin, and defeated death once and for all. Then He in turn gave that victory to you and made you a victorious conqueror with hope beyond the grave. What an astounding summary of what Jesus accomplished for you! Now, you simply accept God's Grace by faith to live a victorious life.

Taking Action For Victory.

What is one thing from this verse that God is affirming to you right now?

_____

_____

_____

After meditating on this verse, how does it inspire you to re-evaluate your faith journey so you can walk in victory?

_____

_____

_____

How will you apply this verse to your life so you can begin walking in victory or rise to a higher level of victory in your life?

_____

_____

_____

Day 9

Rise Up In Glorious Splendor

Rise up in splendor and be radiant, for your light has dawned, and Yahweh's glory now streams from you! Isaiah 60:1

Sweet child of mine, are you overcome with feelings of despair and hopelessness today because of your temporary condition? Do you want to hide yourself from the world by staying in bed all day?

You are My child. I love you. I created you to not only overcome life's circumstances, but to thrive and continuously live in victory. I am not going to allow you to stay depressed. It is time to rise up and throw off the covers of despair and depression.

Open the curtains on your darkness and allow My glorious light to shine in upon you. Put your face to the sunshine. Feel the warmth of My love. Look up. Look around. Think about My goodness and My Glory enveloping you today.

Allow yourself to feel and experience My goodness shining on you, enveloping every part of your being. Permit My Holy Spirit to wash over you renewing your thoughts and refreshing your soul. It is a new day. It is time to rise up and let My Glory shine through you for all the world to see.

Prayer - *Lord, in the authority of the Name of Jesus, I bind the Spirit of Depression that tries to hold me captive and I loose it from its assignment against me. I am changing my position and seeking Your face. I am allowing Your Glory and Your goodness to envelope me right now. Thank You for helping me rise up to let my light shine in the world.*

Thoughts to Ponder.

If you want change in your life, you must be willing to be the change you desire. Today is your day to choose to rise up from old mindsets of depression and despair that have held you captive due to your circumstances. Every day, opportunities of life and death come to you. God says choose life and rise up to a new life by reading God's Word to be radiant with His glory.

Taking Action For Victory.

What is one thing from this verse that God is affirming to you right now?

_____

_____

_____

After meditating on this verse, how does it inspire you to re-evaluate your faith journey so you can walk in victory?

_____

_____

_____

How will you apply this verse to your life so you can begin walking in victory or rise to a higher level of victory in your life?

_____

_____

_____

Day 10

You Are Rising Up Victorious

For the lovers of God may suffer adversity and stumble seven times, but they will continue to rise over and over again. Proverbs 24:16a

Where are you in your life today? Do you think you are knocked down with a final blow suffering adversity, or are you in the process of rising again, overcoming your enemy's attacks?

I encourage you with this My precious child, it does not matter what your adversary brings to criticize or attack you. He may have hit you with a blow so strong it knocks the wind out of your sails. Regardless, you are My child, and you will not be crushed.

Today is your day to look yourself in the mirror and affirm to yourself and the world that you will not be denied or defeated. The enemy may have hit you again and again with his best shot, but you are My champion.

You are getting up more determined and more resilient to take your rightful place of authority enforcing Satan's defeat.

Prayer - *Thank You, Father that I am Your child, and I cannot be defeated. Regardless of what my situation looks like right now, You tell me I will rise above it. I believe and I receive Your promise right now in Jesus Name. Lord, although I may have fallen, I ask You to help me rise again. I will not quit or be denied restoration of everything Satan has stolen from me.*

Thoughts to Ponder.

Failure is never final in God's eyes. Many times, failure leads you to your greatest adventure, one that you would otherwise not take a step of faith to pursue. A business disaster, a broken relationship, or a health setback does not define who you are. There is a time to process your setbacks, and a time to get back up, dust yourself off, and thank God for courage to begin again.

Taking Action For Victory.

What is one thing from this verse that God is affirming to you right now?

_____

_____

_____

After meditating on this verse, how does it inspire you to re-evaluate your faith journey so you can walk in victory?

_____

_____

_____

How will you apply this verse to your life so you can begin walking in victory or rise to a higher level of victory in your life?

_____

_____

_____

Day 11

Your Accusers Are Silenced

So now, the case is closed. There remains no accusing voice of condemnation against those who are joined in life-union with Jesus, the Anointed One. Romans 8:1

My beloved one, your flesh has no claim on you, and you have no further obligation to live in obedience to it. My Holy Spirit imparts life to you because you are fully accepted by Me.

In the past, your lofty desires to do what is good were destroyed when you did the very things you wanted to avoid. Then your conscience condemned you and confirmed the power of the Law in your life.

My child, Jesus now lives His life in you. Where you once lived under the Law that empowered your sinful desires, you are now fully released from that power, and it no longer controls you. Your life is no longer motivated by following the Law because now you desire to serve Me by living in the freshness of a new life empowered by the Holy Spirit.

Your renewed mind is fixed on and submitted to My righteous principles that bring you My abundant life.

Prayer – *Father, I ask You to give me a greater revelation of Jesus providing the way of escape from sin for me. I ask You to help me focus my mind on Your Word to realize I am righteous. There are no longer any condemning accusations against me. Living my life surrendered to Your Holy Spirit puts to death the corrupt ways of my flesh.*

Thoughts to Ponder.

Do you realize that even when you want to do good, evil is ready to sabotage you? You love God and desire to do what pleases Him, and yet you recognize there is another power operating within you, waging war against your mind, trying to bring you into captivity. Jesus, the Anointed One, has power to rescue you from the unwelcome intruder of sin and death.

Taking Action For Victory.

What is one thing from this verse that God is affirming to you right now?

_____

_____

_____

After meditating on this verse, how does it inspire you to re-evaluate your faith journey so you can walk in victory?

_____

_____

_____

How will you apply this verse to your life so you can begin walking in victory or rise to a higher level of victory in your life?

_____

_____

_____

Day 12

Sing Your Victory Song

Go ahead—sing your brand-new song to the Lord! He is famous for his miracles and marvels, for he is victorious through his mighty power and holy strength. Psalm 98:1

My chosen one, now is the time to lift your voice and sing your victory song! Do not focus on your circumstances. Instead, as an act of your faith, shout unto Me with a voice of triumph

You know My voice and you read My words to you. They are words of truth, and they bring you much comfort in your life.

My child, I am protecting you and keeping you from Satan's power. You cannot be defeated. When you became My child, I made you triumphant. I reveal My goodness to you. I give you reason to celebrate My wonderful miracles in your life.

I always demonstrate My lovingkindness and faithfulness to you. This gives you great reason to rejoice and celebrate.

Throw off the discouragement and despair caused by things that do not go the way you anticipated and be resolute in your praise to Me. Sing with your new victory song!

Prayer - *Father I ask You to help me see beyond my temporary circumstances to the marvelous victory You have given me. Because I am Your child, I cannot be defeated. Thank You for protecting me from the evil and wickedness in this world. You have always been faithful to me. I celebrate and rejoice with a new victory song in my heart that I sing to You.*

Thoughts to Ponder.

Sing your victory song today with boldness! Yes, sing in the middle of your chaos and watch God turn things around for you. When you sing praises, you are entering into spiritual warfare and confusing your enemy. He is trying to discourage and defeat you, and you are singing God's highest praises. God has already given you the victory so you should go ahead and celebrate.

Taking Action For Victory.

What is one thing from this verse that God is affirming to you right now?

_____

_____

_____

After meditating on this verse, how does it inspire you to re-evaluate your faith journey so you can walk in victory?

_____

_____

_____

How will you apply this verse to your life so you can begin walking in victory or rise to a higher level of victory in your life?

_____

_____

_____

Day 13

Your Enemy Is Defeated

I write these things to you, dear children, because you truly have a relationship with the Father. I write these things, fathers and mothers, because you have had a true relationship with him who is from the beginning. And I write these things, young people, because you are strong, the Word of God is treasured in your hearts, and you have defeated the Evil One. 1 John 2:14

You will always be My child, regardless of what age you are today. Your sins have been permanently removed from you because of the power of the Name of Jesus.

The most important thing in your life today is having a relationship with Me, My Son, and My Holy Spirit. However, there are three main elements to your spiritual growth. These are your courageous faith, your love for My Word, and you enforcing your enemy's defeat through your life union with Jesus.

You have a genuine relationship with Us regardless of your age. Therefore, your enemy, Satan, is defeated because you share in Jesus's triumph over the cross and His resurrection from the dead. You overcome Satan by the Blood of Jesus and the word of His testimony. These cause you to be victorious.

Prayer - *Thank You, Father, for defeating the enemy for me through the shed Blood of Jesus, I can now walk in total victory regardless of my age. I thank You that Jesus is my Savior and I ask You to give me courageous faith to step out and do what You ask me to do. I ask You to give me more desire to read Your Word and know your ways more intimately.*

Thoughts to Ponder.

God longs to have intimacy with you, so He sent Jesus to bridge the gap and defeat Satan once and for all. You are strong in the Lord and the power of His might. God's Word is a treasure to your heart as you read it, study it, and meditate on it so you can hide it in your heart. As God's child, you were created to enforce Satan's defeat in your life and walk in total victory.

Taking Action For Victory.

What is one thing from this verse that God is affirming to you right now?

_____

_____

_____

After meditating on this verse, how does it inspire you to re-evaluate your faith journey so you can walk in victory?

_____

_____

_____

How will you apply this verse to your life so you can begin walking in victory or rise to a higher level of victory in your life?

_____

_____

_____

Day 14

The Lord Fights For You

For the Lord your God is going with you! He will fight for you against your enemies, and he will give you victory! Deuteronomy 20:4 – NLT

My child, as you go out to perform your responsibilities today, know that My Holy Spirit goes before you and with you. I am your Father, and I care for you.

Throughout your day, you will have many opportunities to celebrate My goodness. However, there may be things that you dread because you know the enemy is fighting against you.

Although your enemy does not come at you with horses and chariots as in Bible times, I realize your enemies are just as real and intimidating to you today as they were to My children back then.

Settle in your heart right now that I am with you, and I will bring you out of every contrary situation just like I brought My children out of Egypt. Do not be afraid. I am your Lord, and I am with you! You can trust me to bring you into victory!

Prayer – *Father God, thank You for being my loving Father. Please help me realize You are always for me. You are with me. You never leave me defenseless. I ask You to give me courage to trust You in the heat of my battles, and to know that You always deliver me from the hands of my enemy. I thank You in advance for leading me into victory.*

Thoughts to Ponder.

Do not lose heart, panic, or tremble in the face of your enemy. God has delivered you from his hand and given you the victory over him, because He sent Jesus to pay the price for your victory. Jesus in turn gave you His authority and His victory over Satan. The Holy Spirit goes before you and fights all your battles for you. You can trust God because He is always faithful.

Taking Action For Victory.

What is one thing from this verse that God is affirming to you right now?

_____

_____

_____

After meditating on this verse, how does it inspire you to re-evaluate your faith journey so you can walk in victory?

_____

_____

_____

How will you apply this verse to your life so you can begin walking in victory or rise to a higher level of victory in your life?

_____

_____

_____

Day 15

Who Can Stand Against You

So, what does all this mean? If God has determined to stand with us, tell me, who then could ever stand against us? Romans 8:31

You may feel the pressure of enemy forces attacking you, but be encouraged today, My faithful child. Every detail of your life is continually woven together for good because I have chosen you in love to be Mine. You can be assured that any suffering you are currently enduring is nothing compared to the magnitude of My Glory that is about to be unveiled within you.

I have proven My deep love for you by giving you My greatest treasure, the gift of My Precious Son, Jesus. Since I freely offered Him up as the sacrifice for you, I will not withhold any good thing from you.

Jesus gave His life for you, conquered death for you, and is now seated at My right hand continually interceding for your victory. My Holy Spirit empowers you in your weakness as Jesus intercedes on your behalf, pleading to Me with emotional sighs too deep for words.

Prayer – *Father God, thank You for giving me Your most precious gifts of Jesus and Your Holy Spirit. You gave me Your Precious Son, so I am confident that You will not withhold any good thing from me. Lord, I ask You to help me remember they are always with me; they are always praying for me and leading me into victory. Nothing can stand against me.*

Thoughts to Ponder.

God is always standing with you. There is nothing in this world or no one that can ever separate you from the endless love of Father God. Nothing in the universe has the power to diminish His love for you. Troubles, persecutions, pressures, problems, deprivations, dangers, death threats; none of these are capable of coming between you and God's omnipotent love for you.

Taking Action For Victory.

What is one thing from this verse that God is affirming to you right now?

_____

_____

_____

After meditating on this verse, how does it inspire you to re-evaluate your faith journey so you can walk in victory?

_____

_____

_____

How will you apply this verse to your life so you can begin walking in victory or rise to a higher level of victory in your life?

_____

_____

_____

Day 16

Celebrate And Shout For Joy

When you succeed, we will celebrate and shout for joy. Flags will fly when victory is yours! Yes, God will answer your prayers, and we will praise him! Psalm 20:5

Do not be discouraged when you experience great perils My child. Stop what you are doing and celebrate your victory! Shout for joy with a voice of triumph and thank Me for what I am doing in you and through you.

Yes, cry out to Me in your chaos and uncertainty. Then listen. I am answering you, delivering you and setting you safely in your high place.

Your enemies will not prevail over you. They will disintegrate in defeat as you rise up full of courage and fight the good fight of faith.

I have given you My supernatural power and every spiritual gift that you need to walk in victory.

Your strength is found in My miracle working power to deliver you from the hand of the enemy. Wave your victory flag, celebrate, and praise Me because I have given you your victory!

Prayer – *Father, thank You for delivering me from my enemies and giving me the victory. I ask you to help me renew my mind with Your Word to know this truth. Remind me that Jesus paid the price for me to walk in victory over my adversary, and the only battle I fight now is the fight of faith. Thank You for supernatural help to fulfill Your plan for my life.*

Thoughts to Ponder.

All of God's promises to you are *Yes and Amen*. He gives you all the things you ask for and He brings you victory because you are His anointed child. Release your faith and receive His promises today. God's deliverance cry over you is heard across heaven and His miracles are manifesting through His mighty hand and His strength. Wave your victory flag and celebrate!

Taking Action For Victory.

What is one thing from this verse that God is affirming to you right now?

_____

_____

_____

After meditating on this verse, how does it inspire you to re-evaluate your faith journey so you can walk in victory?

_____

_____

_____

How will you apply this verse to your life so you can begin walking in victory or rise to a higher level of victory in your life?

_____

_____

_____

Day 17

The Lord Is For You

So we can say with great confidence: "I know the Lord is for me and I will never be afraid of what people may do to me!" Hebrews 13:6

My dear child, do not be obsessed with the lust of your flesh, the lust of your eyes, money, or earthly riches. I would rather you live your life trusting Me, being content with what you have and resting in My presence.

Your greatest joy is found as you live your life in My presence, communing with Me. I have promised you that I will never leave you nor forsake you. I will always be with you, and I will never loosen My grip on you.

I am for you, not against you. You do not have to be in fear of what people may try to do to you because I am your Protector and Provider.

If you want an example of how to live a life of victory, look at Jesus and how He lived His life. He walked by faith to accomplish the things I ask Him to do. Now you have the power to live your life walking in faith because it is your victory.

Prayer – *Father, Thank You that I can confidently say You will never leave me, abandon me, or loosen your grip on me. Thank You that You are for me and not against me. I ask You to help me guard my eyes and my flesh from lusting after things in this world that will not satisfy me. Help me build my faith by hearing Your Word so I can walk in victory.*

Thoughts to Ponder.

Jesus is the same yesterday, today and forever. The Holy Spirit is always with you, and He will never leave you. Because He is your Helper and your Protector, you do not need to concern yourself about what people say about you or what they try to do to you. You can walk by faith, putting your trust in God's Word as you are strengthened spiritually to live a victorious life.

Taking Action For Victory.

What is one thing from this verse that God is affirming to you right now?

_____

_____

_____

After meditating on this verse, how does it inspire you to re-evaluate your faith journey so you can walk in victory?

_____

_____

_____

How will you apply this verse to your life so you can begin walking in victory or rise to a higher level of victory in your life?

_____

_____

_____

Day 18

God Will Defeat Your Enemy

With God's help, we will fight like heroes, and he will trample down our every foe! Psalm 60:12

I have not walked away from you or left you defenseless, My dear child. I am right here with you. I am doing miraculous signs and wonders for you because I love you. Come running to Me and allow Me to pour My love out over you.

Do not try to fight your battle in your own strength. I am strengthening you with My power and My might as you stand in faith against your enemy. I am here with you, fighting your battles for you in opposition to your enemies. With My help, you are enforcing Satan's defeat in your life, and I am trampling down all your foes.

You are My servant and I promise you that in your heroic triumph I am pouring out My inheritance on you so you can receive everything I have vowed to give you.

You are My special warrior and I rejoice over you at your victory.

Prayer – *Father, thank You for not leaving me defenseless against Satan's attacks. I am not moved by how I feel or by what is happening in my life right now. I ask You to help me see that You have already defeated my enemies and given me the victory because as Jesus is so am I. Thank You for fighting all my battles as I stay in faith and rest in believing Your Word.*

Thoughts to Ponder.

God hears you when you cry out to Him in despair in the heat of your battle. He is right there with you holding your hand. His lovingkindness and truth are leading you into victory. As you trust Him to help you, you will never be disappointed in His faithfulness to keep His promises to you. He is singing over you with songs of deliverance and rejoicing with you in your victory.

Taking Action For Victory.

What is one thing from this verse that God is affirming to you right now?

_____

_____

_____

_____

After meditating on this verse, how does it inspire you to re-evaluate your faith journey so you can walk in victory?

_____

_____

_____

How will you apply this verse to your life so you can begin walking in victory or rise to a higher level of victory in your life?

_____

_____

_____

Day 19

You Have Mighty Power

For God will never give you the spirit of fear, but the Holy Spirit who gives you mighty power, love, and self-control.
2 Timothy 1:7

You are My cherished child. I would like to announce to you this wonderful promise of life that is only available to you through My Anointed Son, Jesus.

Many times, you have been fearful to step out in faith and to do what I have created you to do. Please realize that I have not given you a spirit of fear. This comes from Satan, your enemy. Satan wants to paralyze you and keep you from living a fulfilling life.

I have given you the gift of My Holy Spirit, and He gives you His mighty power. I have given you a heart full of love, and self-control, self-discipline, and a sound mind so you can walk in victory.

I give you resurrection power to overcome every attack of your enemy by the revelation of My Holy Spirit's power working in you to equip you to live the victorious life.

Prayer – *Father, I am so grateful You did not give me a spirit of fear. Thank You for giving me the promise of Your Holy Spirit when Jesus ascended back to Heaven. I ask You to help me stir up the spiritual gifts You have given me. I believe I receive Your Holy Spirit's power to overcome fear with a sound* mind to live a self-disciplined life so I can live victoriously.

Thoughts to Ponder.

Imagine yourself using your spiritual gifts to live a fearless, self-disciplined life, full of God's love, and totally trusting in His Grace. God has given you a sound mind and you can live a valiant, courageous life without limits through the Holy Spirit's power living on the inside of you. He empowers your life and dismantles every aspect of death so you can live victoriously.

Taking Action For Victory.

What is one thing from this verse that God is affirming to you right now?

_____

_____

_____

After meditating on this verse, how does it inspire you to re-evaluate your faith journey so you can walk in victory?

_____

_____

_____

How will you apply this verse to your life so you can begin walking in victory or rise to a higher level of victory in your life?

_____

_____

_____

Day 20

Your Power Conquers Difficulties

And I find that the strength of Christ's explosive power infuses me to conquer every difficulty. Philippians 4:13

My dear and precious child, I love you so deeply. You are truly a glorious joy to My heart. Now is your time to shine in the fullness of your unity with Me. It is time to celebrate with great joy the victories you have won in this season of your life. Let your joy overflow out of you onto those around you.

Instead of being pulled in different directions or worried about the various things in your life, relax, continue to saturate yourself in My Presence, and pray throughout your day.

You will find peace as you bring your faith-filled prayer requests to Me along with your overflowing gratitude of what I have done for you.

You can be satisfied in all of life's circumstances. If you are experiencing overwhelming abundance or overcoming temporary lack, you can be assured that through the strength of My Holy Spirit's explosive power in you, you are overcoming all the things that hinder you. His power enables you to conquer every difficulty in your life.

Prayer - *Thank You, Father God, for filling me with Your overcoming, conquering power of Your Holy Spirit living on the inside of me. He enables me to triumph over all the attacks of the enemy and the difficulties he brings into my life. I ask You to help me be more sensitive to Your Holy Spirit's power in my life so I can enforce Satan's defeat and live a victorious life.*

Thoughts to Ponder.

It does not matter the circumstances you find yourself living in today, God will fully satisfy every want, need, or desire of your heart. You can see the abundant riches of God's glory revealed through Jesus as He walked this earth. Whether you live in abundance or difficulties, the Holy Spirit's power in you empowers you to be content regardless of your circumstances. His power equips you to live victoriously.

Taking Action For Victory.

What is one thing from this verse that God is affirming to you right now?

_____

_____

_____

After meditating on this verse, how does it inspire you to re-evaluate your faith journey so you can walk in victory?

_____

_____

_____

How will you apply this verse to your life so you can begin walking in victory or rise to a higher level of victory in your life?

_____

_____

_____

Day 21

Rest In Great Confidence

And everything I've taught you is so that the peace which is in me will be in you and will give you great confidence as you rest in me. For in this unbelieving world you will experience trouble and sorrows, but you must be courageous, for I have conquered the world! John 16:33

My child, I adore you. Be strong and courageous as you face the world today with its troubles and sorrows. Your older brother, Jesus, My Anointed Son, has destroyed the power this world has over you to defeat you. He has conquered it for you.

Now you can come boldly into the Throne Room of Grace and ask Me directly for anything you want, need or desire and I will give it to you because of your loving relationship with My Son, Jesus.

Because you love My Son and believe that I sent Him to restore our relationship, you can know that My Heart for you is that you receive what you ask of Me so that your joy will be complete and running over with no limits.

You can be courageous and rest with the same peace in your heart that Jesus had in His heart knowing that His victory over Satan is your victory over Satan.

Prayer – *Father, thank You for Your Peace. Thank You for sending Jesus to conquer Satan once and for all when He died on the cross and rose again so our relationship could be restored. I ask You to give me courage to enter into rest, and confidence to know the finished work of Jesus on the cross is my victory. Thank You for Your Holy Spirit's power to stay in peace.*

Thoughts to Ponder.

Although you may experience troubles in your life, you can relax and put your confident trust in the finished work of Jesus on the cross. He died, was buried, rose again, ascended into Heaven, and sat down at the right hand of Father God which is the place of victory. He defeated Satan once and for all, then He gave you the same authority and victory. As Jesus is, so are you.

Taking Action For Victory.

What is one thing from this verse that God is affirming to you right now?

_____

_____

_____

After meditating on this verse, how does it inspire you to re-evaluate your faith journey so you can walk in victory?

_____

_____

_____

How will you apply this verse to your life so you can begin walking in victory or rise to a higher level of victory in your life?

_____

_____

_____

Day 22

You Have Supernatural Help

I am Yahweh, your mighty God! I grip your right hand and won't let you go! I whisper to you: 'Don't be afraid; I am here to help you!' Isaiah 41:13

My favorite child, I chose you before the foundation of the world. Because you are My child, you are the seed of My beloved friend Abraham. I have drawn you to Myself and I want you to know that I have chosen you. I did not reject you.

I am your faithful Father and I do not want you to yield to fear. I am always with you. I infuse you with My strength and help you in every situation you are facing. I am holding you firmly with My victorious right hand.

Do not be in fear about those who rant and rave against you, for they will be put to shame and disgraced. The people who contend or oppose you will perish and disappear. The search for your enemies will be pointless and those who war against you will vanish without a trace! You are My child, and I am taking care for you. You have nothing to fear because I am here to give you victory.

Prayer - *Thank you, Father that I am Your child, and You uphold me with Your victorious right hand. I come boldly into the Throne Room of Grace and ask You to help me remember that I have nothing to fear because You chose me. You are with me and are drawing me to Yourself. Thank You for giving me strength and helping me be victorious in every situation I face.*

Thoughts to Ponder.

God has a strong grip on your hand and is holding it with His victorious right hand. He loves you and is not going to let your hand go. Can you imagine your hand in His strong hand? You have His security and protection right now. He chose you to be His child. You have nothing to fear in life because Father God is holding you close. His desire for you is that you live victoriously.

Taking Action For Victory.

What is one thing from this verse that God is affirming to you right now?

_____

_____

_____

After meditating on this verse, how does it inspire you to re-evaluate your faith journey so you can walk in victory?

_____

_____

_____

How will you apply this verse to your life so you can begin walking in victory or rise to a higher level of victory in your life?

_____

_____

_____

Day 23

God Is Always Faithful To You

We all experience times of testing, which is normal for every human being. But God will be faithful to you. He will screen and filter the severity, nature, and timing of every test or trial you face so that you can bear it. And each test is an opportunity to trust him more, for along with every trial, God has provided for you a way of escape that will bring you out of it victoriously.
1 Corinthians 10:13

My cherished child, I ask you to carefully consider what I am telling you. Do not think it is strange that you are facing various tests, temptations, and trials in your life. Everyone goes through challenges, and you would be foolish to think you were exempt from going through them yourself.

The key to overcoming and living in victory is building your character by what you learn as you go through the various hardships in your life.

However, My faithfulness and grace limit the severity of every test, trial, or temptation you encounter and prevents you from being tested beyond your ability to survive. My unlimited grace is available to you as you face the hardship, temptations, or seasons of difficulty. I made you a victorious overcomer.

Prayer – *Lord, I ask You to help me trust in Your faithfulness as You build a strong character within me and teach me not to fail or give up in the middle of the test, trial, or temptation. Father, I thank You for Your grace that limits the severity of each test and makes a way of escape that empowers me to overcome every difficulty I experience so I can walk in victory.*

Thoughts to Ponder.

Temptations, tests, and trials are just as much a part of life as is the celebration of victory. God did not tell you that every difficulty would be removed from your life; however, you have the resources within you to overcome a challenge of the enemy. God's grace and His faithfulness provide you a way of escape so you will be empowered to endure and be refined in the process.

Taking Action For Victory.

What is one thing from this verse that God is affirming to you right now?

_____

_____

_____

After meditating on this verse, how does it inspire you to re-evaluate your faith journey so you can walk in victory?

_____

_____

_____

How will you apply this verse to your life so you can begin walking in victory or rise to a higher level of victory in your life?

_____

_____

_____

Day 24

You Capture Every Thought

We can demolish every deceptive fantasy that opposes God and break through every arrogant attitude that is raised up in defiance of the true knowledge of God. We capture, like prisoners of war, every thought and insist that it bow in obedience to the Anointed One. 2 Corinthians 10:5

My child, I created you to live a victorious life full of joy and peace. You are not designed to allow negative, defeating thoughts to run wild or torment you in your mind.

I challenge you to resolve yourself to the truth that you are not living by the world's standards. I made you to be led by My Holy Spirit's wisdom and power.

Although you live in this natural world, you do not engage in spiritual battles with human weapons or by using manipulation to achieve your goals.

Your spiritual weapons are empowered by My divine power to destroy all of Satan's schemes. His plan is to hold you captive through faulty thought patterns that defy My authority in your life. He lies to you, steals from you, and destroys you through your thoughts.

You are the only one that can control deceptive thoughts in your mind and make them come into obedience to My Word.

Prayer – *Father, thank You for giving me Your power to dismantle every deceptive fantasy, or lofty thought that is contrary to Your will, and I destroy every scheme of the enemy with Your power. It is in the authority of the Name of Jesus that I break the power of Satan's strongholds in my mind that are formed against the will of God. I am taking every thought captive.*

Thoughts to Ponder.

You are empowered by God's grace and His Word to dismantle every stronghold in your mind. You have the ability to demolish arguments, opinions, theories, and philosophies that are contrary to God's Word. By taking every negative thought captive to the will of God, you are standing ready and willing to engage a spiritual war and defeat the enemy's lies in your life.

Taking Action For Victory.

What is one thing from this verse that God is affirming to you right now?

_____

_____

_____

After meditating on this verse, how does it inspire you to re-evaluate your faith journey so you can walk in victory?

_____

_____

_____

How will you apply this verse to your life so you can begin walking in victory or rise to a higher level of victory in your life?

_____

_____

_____

Day 25

Live Your Life In Total Faith-Rest

So then we must be eager to experience this faith-rest life, so that no one falls short by following the same pattern of doubt and unbelief. Hebrews 4:11

My dearly esteemed child, stop toiling in your own abilities and step over into My promise to you of entering into My rest with your faith. You can embrace the fullness of My promises to you by releasing your faith to receive them.

My works have all been finished from the foundation of the world and I rested from my works on the seventh day.

Do not allow yourself to have a hardened, unbelieving heart that doubts My promises to you for they are still full of power.

When you believe what I tell you, your faith activates My power to produce a harvest in your life. You then experience the realm of confident rest!

Take advantage of this opportunity to enter into My faith-rest life. Cease striving from your own works and celebrate living a life lived by faith. Enter into My rest, just as I celebrated My finished works and rested in them.

Prayer – *Father God, I ask You to help me cease striving from my own works and enter into Your rest. Thank You that I do not have a hardened heart of doubt and unbelief regarding Your promises to me. I am releasing my faith and I believe I receive the promises of Your finished works. I am using my faith to enter into Your rest*

Thoughts to Ponder.

The fact remains that you still have the opportunity to enter into the faith-rest life and experience the fulfillment of God's promises to you. God has still ordained a day for you to enter into His rest and that day is called "Today." You can use your faith today to cling to the truth of God's Word and stand on His promises to enter into His rest.

Taking Action For Victory.

What is one thing from this verse that God is affirming to you right now?

_____

_____

_____

After meditating on this verse, how does it inspire you to re-evaluate your faith journey so you can walk in victory?

_____

_____

_____

How will you apply this verse to your life so you can begin walking in victory or rise to a higher level of victory in your life?

_____

_____

_____

Day 26

You Overcome The Enemy's Power

Now you understand that I have imparted to you my authority to trample over his kingdom. You will trample upon every demon before you and overcome every power Satan possesses. Absolutely nothing will harm you as you walk in this authority. Luke 10:19

I adore you, My child. You have My great power and authority imparted to you because you are My child.

You have power to use My authority and watch demons obey you when you command them in My Son's Name. When you use the Name of Jesus, you are using your authority to trample over Satan and his kingdom.

You are treading upon every demon that comes against you and you overcome every power Satan possesses. There is absolutely nothing that will harm you as you walk in your authority. You topple Satan's world, and he falls defeated in your life.

It pleases My heart to give these revelations to you because you are like a trusting child to Me. My authority is what enables you to enforce Satan's defeat and walk in victory.

Prayer – *Father, thank You for giving me the revelation that I have power and authority to enforce Satan's defeat in my life today. Thank You that I can topple his kingdom with the power of Jesus' Name. I am treading on and tramping all of Satan's powers and there is absolutely nothing in this world that will harm me as I walk in my God-given power and authority.*

Thoughts to Ponder.

Although God has given all of His children His power and authority to use over Satan's schemes, He has hidden this great revelation of His power and authority from those who are proud, and those who think they are wise in their own eyes. He shares this powerful revelation with His children who humble themselves before Him and submit to Him.

Taking Action For Victory.

What is one thing from this verse that God is affirming to you right now?

_____

_____

_____

After meditating on this verse, how does it inspire you to re-evaluate your faith journey so you can walk in victory?

_____

_____

_____

How will you apply this verse to your life so you can begin walking in victory or rise to a higher level of victory in your life?

_____

_____

_____

Day 27

You Are A Partaker Of Victory

God always makes his grace visible in Christ, who includes us as partners of his endless triumph. Through our yielded lives he spreads the fragrance of the knowledge of God everywhere we go. 2 Corinthians 2:14

You are My cherished child and I have given you My grace today through My Son, Jesus Christ. This grace enables you to be a partner in My endless, triumphant victory celebration in your life.

As you live your life yielded to Me, you spread the fragrance of the knowledge of My goodness everywhere you go. You are the unmistakable aroma of My Son's victory. You are life's perfume to those accepting Him as their Savior.

I empower you to overcome by My Holy Spirit as you live your life. I have called you and I have empowered you. You do not need a letter of recommendation to confirm you represent Me. Your very life is your character reference recognized and permanently engraved on the hearts of those you encounter.

Holy Spirit has made you a living letter of My goodness as He has written the pages of your victorious life for all to see.

Prayer - *Thank You, Father God, for giving me Your grace that enables me to be a partner in Your endless, triumphant, victory celebration in my life. I ask You to help me continuously yield my mind, will and emotions to Your plan for my life so I can be a sweet-smelling aroma of Your victory to all those around me that I encounter today.*

Thoughts to Ponder.

By being united with Jesus and His Anointing, you can do anything God asks you to do. Apart from God there is nothing you can do. The Holy Spirit empowers you after God calls you. You have the revelation that you are incapable of doing anything in your own strength. Your true confidence and competence flow from the Holy Spirit's empowering presence.

Taking Action For Victory.

What is one thing from this verse that God is affirming to you right now?

_____

_____

_____

After meditating on this verse, how does it inspire you to re-evaluate your faith journey so you can walk in victory?

_____

_____

_____

How will you apply this verse to your life so you can begin walking in victory or rise to a higher level of victory in your life?

_____

_____

_____

Day 28

You Completely Conquer Satan

They conquered him completely through the blood of the Lamb and the powerful word of his testimony. They triumphed because they did not love and cling to their own lives, even when faced with death. Revelations 12:11

You are My treasured child, and you are more than a conqueror. I made you to overcome Satan just like My Son, Jesus overcame him.

There was a terrible war in heaven and My Archangel, Michael, and his angels fought against Satan, also known as the great dragon. Satan and his angels fought back, but they did not have the power to win, so they could not regain their place in Heaven.

They were thrown out of Heaven forever, being cast down to earth where they still deceive the whole earth today.

Once they were out of Heaven, there was a triumphant voice heard proclaiming that salvation and power were set in place. The kingdom of My reign and the ruling authority of My Son were established.

This is the same power and authority that the Blood of Jesus and His testimony provides for you today to overcome the attacks of Satan and his demonic forces.

Prayer - *Thank You, Father God, that You made me a triumphant conqueror through the Blood of Jesus and His testimony. I ask You to help me remember that You have given me overcoming power and authority, and I can use this power and authority given to me through the Blood and the Name of Jesus to enforce Satan's defeat in my life. He is your defeated foe.*

Thoughts to Ponder.

The accuser of God's children is Satan. He relentlessly accuses them day and night before God's Throne. However, when God's children realize they can enforce Satan's defeat, because not only did the angels defeat him in Heaven, the Blood of Jesus and His testimony are the powerful weapons that continue destroying the works of the devil. This is a victory revelation.

Taking Action For Victory.

What is one thing from this verse that God is affirming to you right now?

_____

_____

_____

After meditating on this verse, how does it inspire you to re-evaluate your faith journey so you can walk in victory?

_____

_____

_____

How will you apply this verse to your life so you can begin walking in victory or rise to a higher level of victory in your life?

_____

_____

_____

Day 29

Divine Strength To Soar

But those who wait for Yahweh's grace will experience divine strength. They will rise up on soaring wings and fly like eagles, run their race without growing weary, and walk through life without giving up. Isaiah 40:31

My precious child, are you weary today? Do you feel faint and exhausted from your massive to-do lists and endless responsibilities?

Come away with Me. Lift up your eyes into the night-time sky. See how I created the universe. I lit every shining star and formed every glowing galaxy. I positioned all of them where they belong. I numbered, counted, and gave every one of them a name. They shine because of My incredible power and awesome might; not one fails to shine!

I took great care when I created them; the same care I used when I created you. I still watch over you. So why would you complain and say that I am not paying attention to your situation, or that I have lost all interest in what happens to you.

If you are weary, I am giving you strength today, and if you are powerless, I am infusing you with increasing strength. If you are feeling faint and exhausted, I am empowering you with my strength today as you wait upon Me.

Prayer – *Father God, thank You, that You took such care and such detail in creating me. Thank You for Your continuous care for me as a loving father. I ask You to infuse me with Your strength, so that I do not grow weary and become powerless. I am waiting upon your strength to lift me up so I can soar on wings like the eagles and run and not be weary.*

Thoughts to Ponder.

When you wait for the Lord's presence to manifest into your presence, you are strengthened with His power. You will not faint. This means God strengthens you as you wait upon Him. The outer court is where you walk. The Holy Place is where you run, and then you soar like eagles into the heavenly realm in the Holy of Holies. Make time today to come into His presence.

Taking Action For Victory.

What is one thing from this verse that God is affirming to you right now?

_____

_____

_____

After meditating on this verse, how does it inspire you to re-evaluate your faith journey so you can walk in victory?

_____

_____

_____

How will you apply this verse to your life so you can begin walking in victory or rise to a higher level of victory in your life?

_____

_____

_____

Day 30

Your Faith Is Your Victory Power

You see, every child of God overcomes the world, for our faith is the victorious power that triumphs over the world.
1 John 5:4

My beloved child, I have made you a champion who overcomes Satan and all of the world's power. You believe that Jesus is the Messiah, and My Child. You confessed Him as your Lord, so you are now my adopted child, and you belong to Me.

Because you love Me, you also love My Son, Jesus. The way to determine your love for Me is by having a passionate love for Me and My children and obeying My commandments. Let me reassure you that My commandments are light. They do not weigh you down with heavy burdens.

Considering you believe Jesus is My Son, you have the living testimony in your heart that I have given you eternal life, and this life has its source in My Son.

You are My child and you continually overcome the world because your faith is the victorious power within you that triumphs over demonic forces in this world. I designed you to be a victorious, world conqueror, defeating all of its power.

Prayer – *Father God, thank You again for confirming that I am Your child. You fashioned me to overcome and triumph over Satan and everything in this world through using my faith. My faith in your Son, Jesus, who is the Messiah, is my victorious power over everything the enemy would try to do to me to hinder or stop me from fulfilling Your call on my life.*

Thoughts to Ponder.

God's message to you is the revelation of faith for salvation. If you publicly declare with your mouth that Jesus is Lord and believe in your heart that God raised Him from the dead, you experience salvation. Your victorious power that overcomes Satan and the evil forces in this world is your faith in God. God created you to enforce Satan's defeat and walk in total victory.

Taking Action For Victory.

What is one thing from this verse that God is affirming to you right now?

_____

_____

_____

After meditating on this verse, how does it inspire you to re-evaluate your faith journey so you can walk in victory?

_____

_____

_____

How will you apply this verse to your life so you can begin walking in victory or rise to a higher level of victory in your life?

_____

_____

_____

Prayer of Salvation

Pray this prayer to be born again and receive Jesus as your Lord and Savior.

Heavenly Father, I come to you in the Name of Jesus. Your Word says, *"If you openly declare that Jesus is Lord and believe in your heart that God raised him from the dead, you will be saved. For it is by believing in your heart that you are made right with God, and it is by openly declaring your faith that you are saved." Romans 10:9-10 NLT.*

I'm calling on You now Jesus. I openly declare that Jesus is Lord, and I believe in my heart that God raised Him from the dead. It is that simple. You are now a born-again child of God.

The Bible says, *"If imperfect parents know how to lovingly take care of their children and give them what they need, how much more will the perfect heavenly Father give the Holy Spirit's fullness when his children ask him." Luke 11:13.*

I'm asking You to fill me with the Holy Spirit. Holy Spirit, rise up within me as I praise God. I expect to speak with other tongues as You give me utterance according to Acts 2:4 which says, *"They were all filled and equipped with the Holy Spirit and were inspired to speak in tongues—empowered by the Spirit to speak in languages they had never learned!"*

Now, worship and praise God as you are filled with the Holy Spirit and speak in your heavenly language, or other tongues.

About Lucia M. Claborn

Lucia Claborn is a victory coach, author, and speaker. She helps people who have been hurt by church, or life, find restoration through building their faith to discover their true identity, so they can walk in victory.

Her heartbeat is to teach people to stand on the Word of God, decree and declare their desired world into existence, and release their faith to receive their heart's desires.

Lucia has been writing for more than 30 years, with her recent books being available on Amazon as well as countless publishing platforms around the world.

Her weekly podcast, Secrets to Victorious Living, encourages listeners around the world by building their faith to walk in victory.

Lucia and her husband Danny live in North Alabama. They have four grown children and three grandchildren. You can find Lucia online at:

LuciaClaborn.com
Instagram: @LuciaClaborn
Clubhouse: Lucia Claborn - Celebrating Victorious Living
Pinterest: Secrets to Victorious Living Podcast

Other Products Available From

Lucia M. Claborn

Books

English Version
ABC's Of Who I Am - Decreeing
Who God Says I Am ABC's Of
Who I Am Journal - Decreeing
Who God Says I Am

Spanish Version
ABC's Of Who I Am - Decreeing
Who God Says I Am ABC's Of Who
I Am Journal - Decreeing Who God
Says I Am

Podcast
Secrets to Victorious Living
Listen On Stitcher, Pinterest, iTunes or
your favorite podcast platform.